2nd grade
writing journal

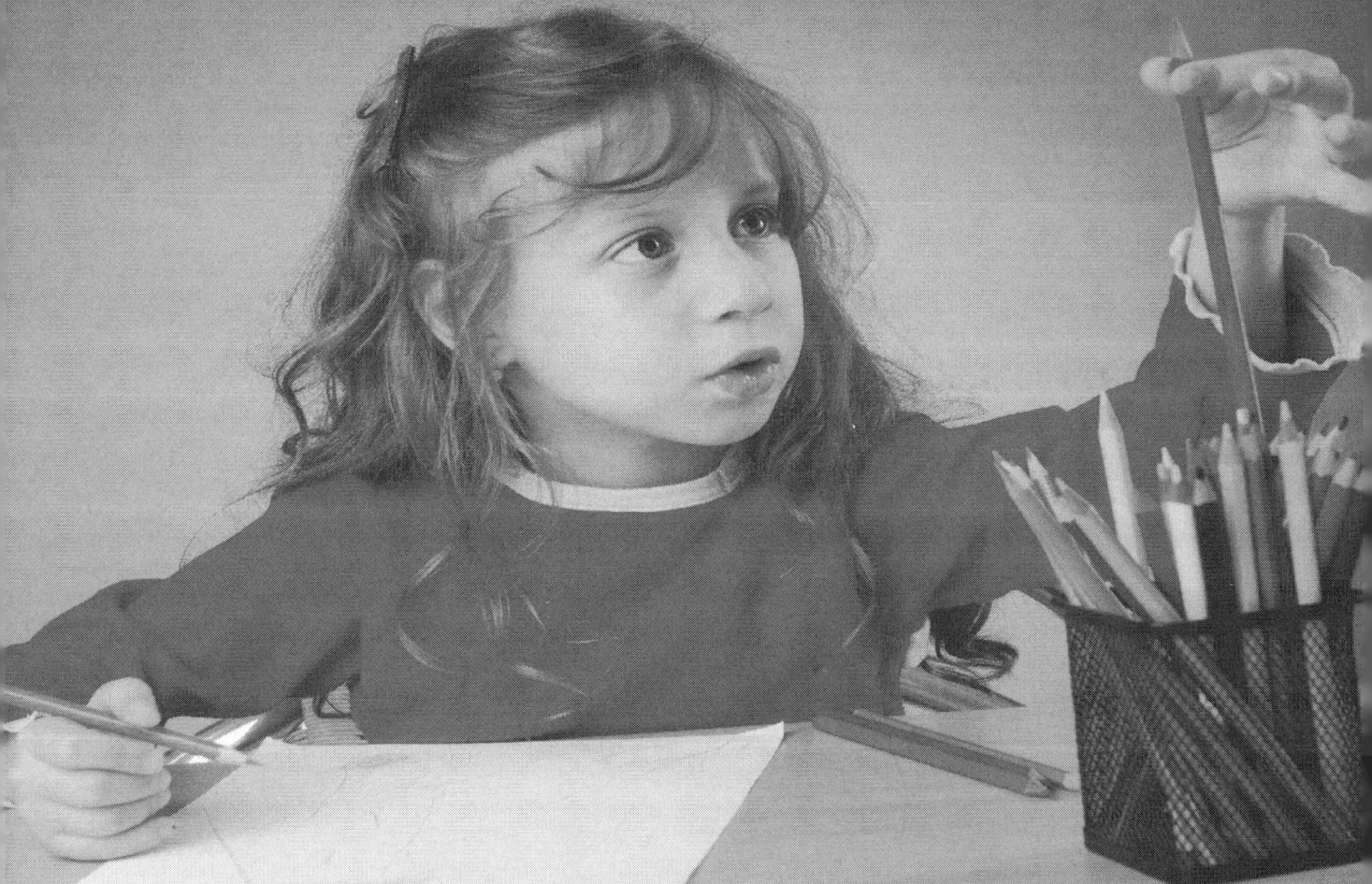

macy mccullough

ISBN 978-1511774574

A SOAR Leadership Company Publication • Grade Level 1-2
SOAR Leadership Company, P.O. Box 481030 | Charlotte, NC 28269

The development of good reading and writing skills is essential not only for success in school but also for success in life. Writing daily will help your student develop their writing skills and practice sentence development, a fundamental key to becoming an excellent writer.

This journal can be used in conjunction with ready-made story-starters or it can be used daily as a tool by student writers to record their daily activities, adventures, imaginative thoughts, etc.

SPELLING
> Students should be encouraged to review their writing when finished and correct spelling errors that may occur with commonly used sight words.

TITLE: _____

TITLE: _____

TITLE: _____

TITLE: _____

TITLE: _____

TITLE: _____

TITLE: _____

TITLE: _____

TITLE: _____

TITLE: _____

TITLE: _____

TITLE: _____

TITLE: _____

TITLE: _____

TITLE: _____

TITLE: _____

TITLE: _____

TITLE: _____

TITLE: _____

TITLE: _____

TITLE: _____

TITLE: _____

TITLE: _____

TITLE: _____

TITLE: _____

TITLE: _____

_____

- -

_____

_____

- -

_____

_____

- -

_____

_____

- -

_____

_____

- -

_____

_____

- -

_____

_____

- -

_____

_____

- -

_____

_____

- -

_____

_____

- -

_____

TITLE: _____

TITLE: _____

TITLE: _____

TITLE: _____

TITLE: _____

TITLE: _____

TITLE: _____

TITLE: _____

TITLE: _____

TITLE: _____

TITLE: _____

TITLE: _____

TITLE: _____

TITLE: _____

TITLE: _____

TITLE: _____

TITLE: _____

TITLE: _____

TITLE: _____

TITLE: _____

TITLE: _____

TITLE: _____

TITLE: _____

TITLE: _____

TITLE: _____

TITLE: _____

TITLE: _____

TITLE: _____

TITLE: _____

TITLE: _____

TITLE: _____

TITLE: _____

TITLE: _____

TITLE: _____

TITLE: _____

TITLE: _____

TITLE: _____

TITLE: _____

TITLE: _____

TITLE: _____

TITLE: _____

TITLE: _____

TITLE: _____

TITLE: _____

TITLE: _____

TITLE: _____

TITLE: _____

TITLE: _____

TITLE: _____

TITLE: _____

TITLE: _____

TITLE: _____

TITLE: _____

TITLE: _____

TITLE: _____

TITLE: _____

TITLE: _____

TITLE: _____

TITLE: _____

TITLE: _____

TITLE: _____

TITLE: _____

TITLE: _____

TITLE: _____

TITLE: _____

TITLE: _____

TITLE: _____

TITLE: _____

TITLE: _____

TITLE: _____

TITLE: _____

TITLE: _____

TITLE: _____

TITLE: _____

Made in the USA
Las Vegas, NV
06 November 2020